THIS BOOK BELONGS TO

. . . .

. . . .

I spy with my little eye, something beginning with...

Aa

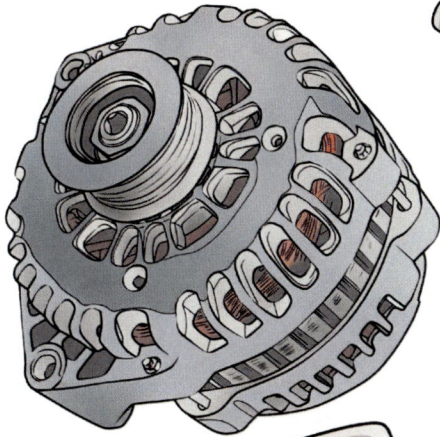

A is for ALTERNATOR

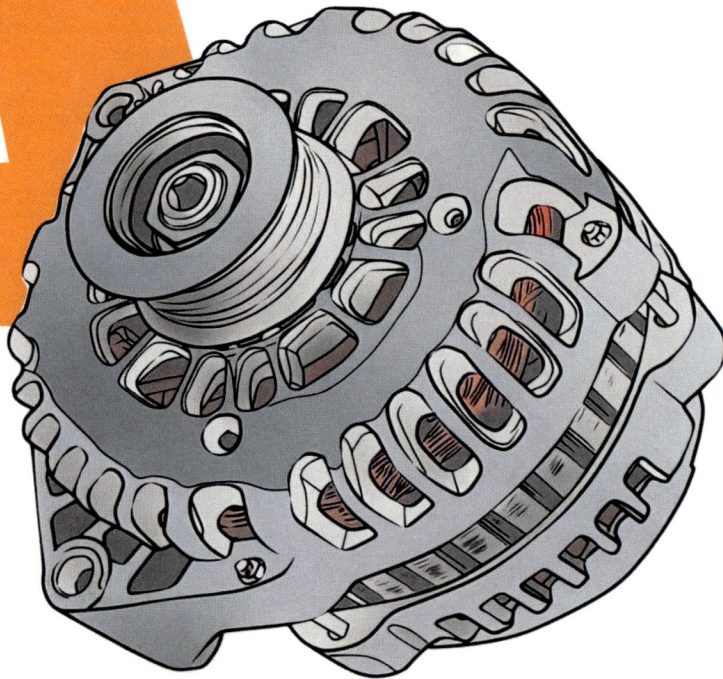

The alternator turns rotation movements to electricity ⚡ that charge the battery 🔋

I spy with my little eye, something beginning with...

Bb

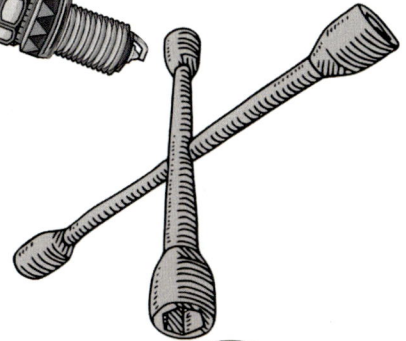

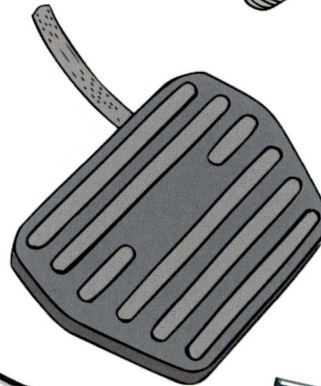

B is for
BRAKE PEDAL

When pressed, the brake pedal activate the braking system that slow down and stop the vehicle.

I spy with my little eye, something beginning with...

Cc

C

is for
CARBURETOR

The carburetor mixes air with fuel and provides the correct fuel/air ratio to the engine.

I spy with my little eye, something beginning with...

D d

D is for DASHBOARD

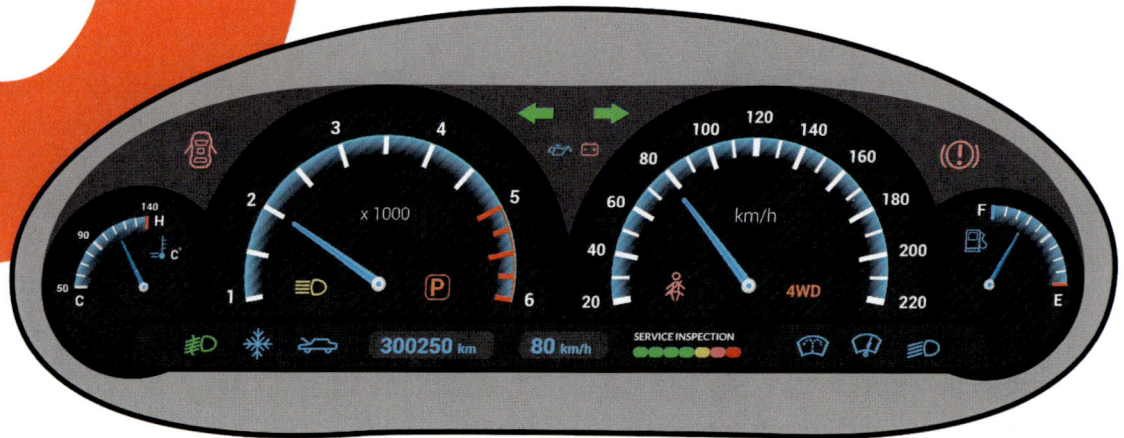

The dashboard displays instrumentation and controls for the vehicle's driver.

I spy with my little eye, something beginning with...

E e

E is for ENGINE

The engine creates the power to move a vehicle by burning either diesel or petrol.

I spy with my little eye, something beginning with...

F f

F is for FILTER

Every car has four main filters: cabin filter, oil filter, fuel filter and air filter. They catch impurities like dust and dirt.

I spy with my little eye, something beginning with...

Gg

G

is for
GEARBOX

The gearbox control the engine torque and power transmission to the wheels.

I spy with my little eye, something beginning with...

Hh

H is for HEADLAMP

The headlamp is attached to the front of the vehicle to illuminate the road ahead.

I spy with my little eye, something beginning with...

Ii

is for
INTERCOOLER

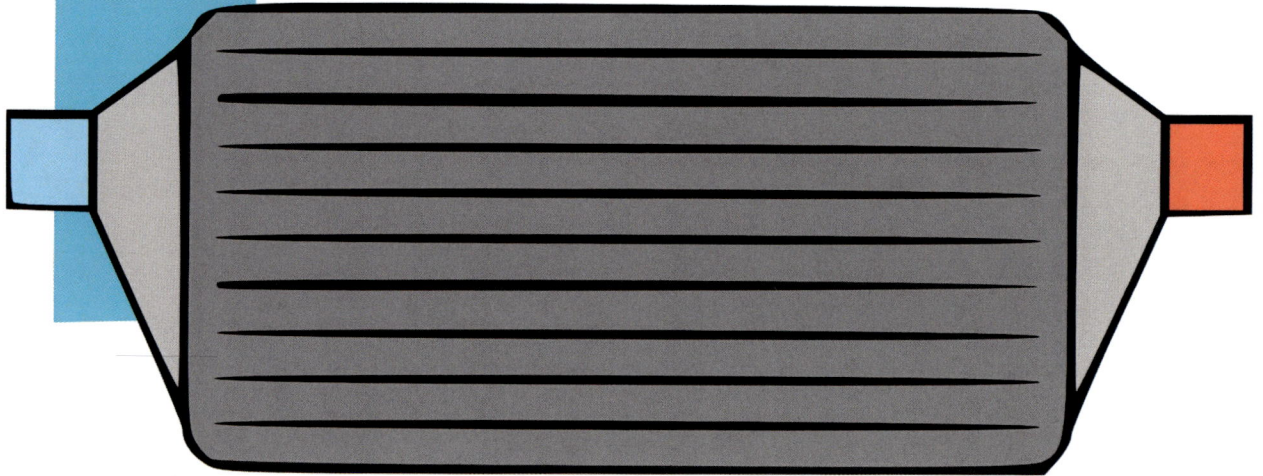

The intercooler cools the air compressed by the turbo/ supercharger.

I spy with my little eye, something beginning with...

Jj

J is for JACK STANDS

The jack stands keep the vehicle from falling to the ground if the lifting jack is removed or faulty.

I spy with my little eye, something beginning with...

Kk

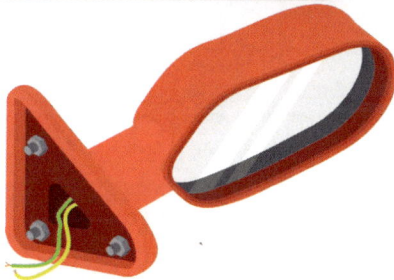

K is for KEY

The car key can open the doors, as well as start the ignition, and also open the trunk (boot) of the car.

I spy with my little eye, something beginning with...

L *l*

L is for LUG WRENCH

The lug wrench is used to loosen and tighten lug nuts on automobile wheels.

I spy with my little eye, something beginning with...

Mm

M is for MUFFLER

The muffler (or silencer) is a device for reducing the noise emitted by the exhaust.

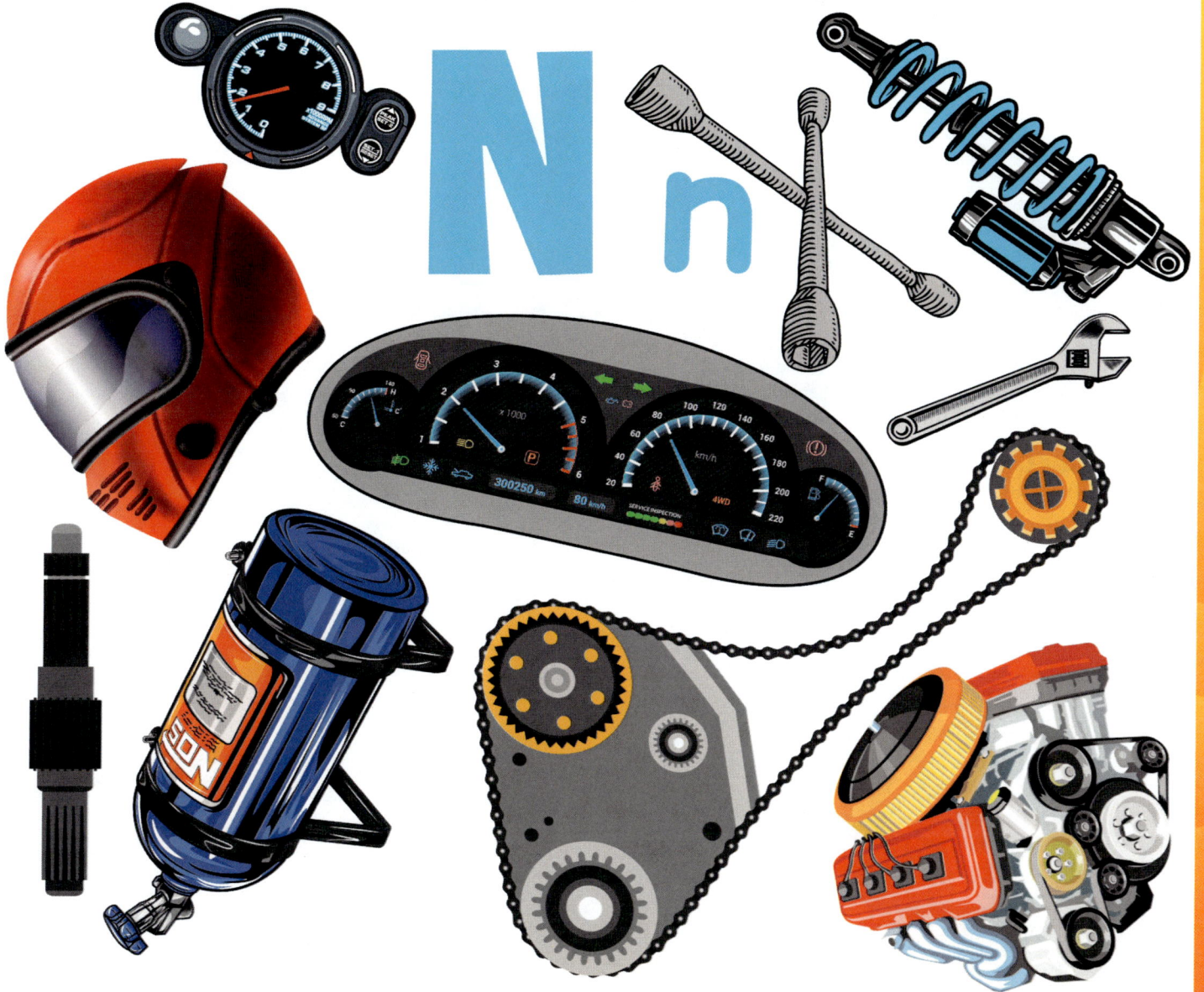

I spy with my little eye, something beginning with...

N n

N is for NITROUS

The nitrous increases the engine's power output by allowing fuel to be burned at a higher-than-normal rate.

I spy with my little eye, something beginning with...

O o

O is for OIL

The oil cleans the engine and keeps it cool and running smoothly.

I spy with my little eye, something beginning with...

P p

P is for PISTON

The piston moves up and down to change the volume of fuel inside a cylinder in the engine, which leads to fuel compression and combustion.

I spy with my little eye, something beginning with...

Q q

Q is for QUAD TURBO ENGINE

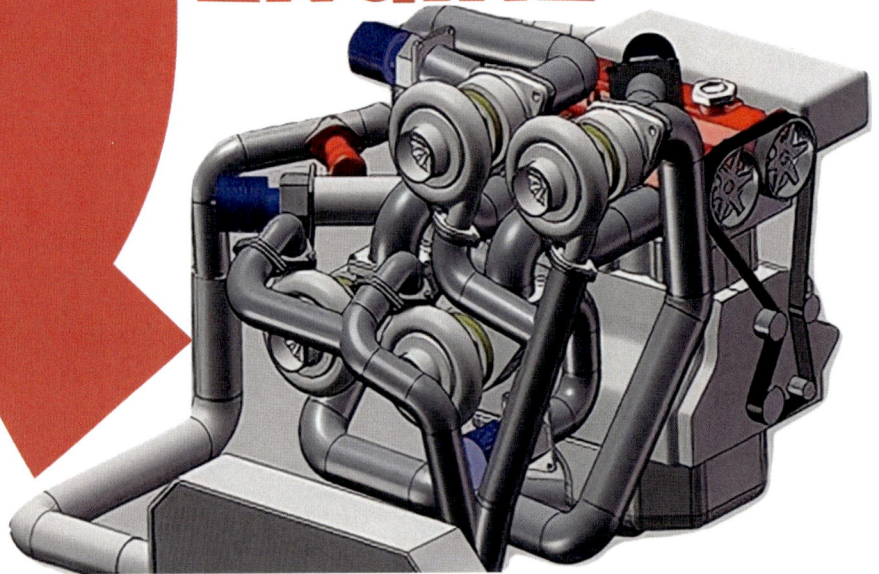

The quad turbo engine is powered by four turbos, the turbo 🌀 is a compressor that forces air into the engine which increase the power.

I spy with my little eye, something beginning with...

R r

R is for ROTOR

The rotor is a part of the braking system, the friction between the rotor and the braking pads slows down the car.

I spy with my little eye, something beginning with...

S s

S is for STEERING WHEEL

The steering wheel allows a driver to control the direction of the vehicle.

I spy with my little eye, something beginning with...

T *t*

T is for TIRES

The tires (tyres) provide traction on the surface so the car can move and travel easily.

I spy with my little eye, something beginning with...

Uu

U is for UNDERCARRIAGE

The undercarriage is the section of a vehicle that is underneath the main cabin of the vehicle.

I spy with my little eye, something beginning with...

V v

V is for VENTS

The vents provide a constant through-flow of fresh air and keep the car at a comfortable temperature.

I spy with my little eye, something beginning with...

W w

W

is for

WHEEL COVER

The wheel cover is used cover the central part of wheels. It prevent dust and other harmful elements from getting into wheels.

I spy with my little eye, something beginning with...

X x

X is for XENON HEADLIGHTS

The xenon headlights emit a whitish-blue light that lights up more of the road than traditional halogen lights.

I spy with my little eye, something beginning with...

Y y

Y is for YOKE

The yoke is a triangular metal piece used to connect the main brake cable with the stirrup cable.

I spy with my little eye, something beginning with...

Z z

Z is for
ZEV

ZEV stands for Zero Emission Vehicles, they are eco-friendly vehicles that never emits exhaust gas from the onboard source of power.

Made in the USA
Middletown, DE
05 May 2022